AF334653

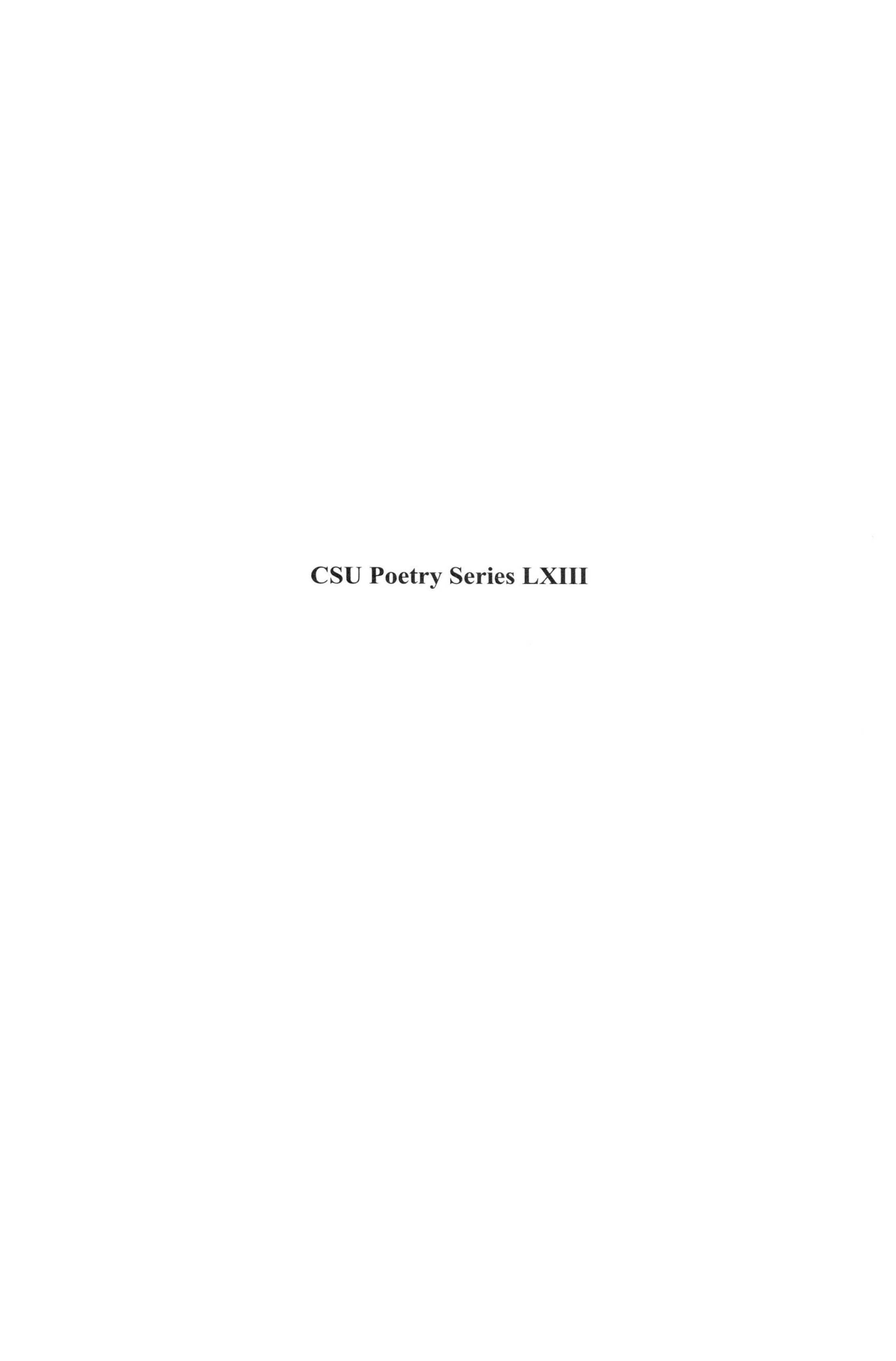

CSU Poetry Series LXIII

Guide to Native Beasts

Mary Quade

Cleveland State University Poetry Center

Acknowledgments

Grateful acknowledgement is made to the following publications,
in which these poems originally appeared:

Chicago Review: "Widowed"
Colorado Review: "Love Archetype"
Columbia: A Journal of Literature and Art: "Tractor"
Crab Orchard Review: "Bats"
The Cream City Review: "Horse Girl"
Epoch: "Tornado"
Field: "Hammer," "Dress"
Fine Madness: "Locomotive"
The Iowa Review: "Episode of Moose"
The Massachusetts Review: "Abandoned House near Hanford
    Nuclear Reservation"
Mid-American Review: "Epitaph"
New Delta Review: "Giant Fiberglass Cow"
The North American Review: "Lunar Eclipse: Hale Bopp over
    Palo Alto"
North Dakota Quarterly: "Air Show: F-16s above Cleveland"
Notre Dame Review: "Lawn Shrines: Bathtub Virgins," "At the
    Costume Shop"
Poet Lore: "Emus"
River Styx: "Chicken"
Sycamore Review: "Herb Morrison Reporting on the
    Hindenburg, May 6, 1937," "Spontaneous Generation"
Tar River Poetry: "Zamboni Man: The Mall"
Willow Springs: "Holly Hobby Dolls"

Thank you also to Literary Arts of Portland, Oregon for a fellow-
ship supporting the completion of this book and to Caldera.
Special thanks to the libraries I have frequented.

Copyright © 2003 by Mary Quade
Published by Cleveland State University Poetry Center
2121 Euclid Avenue
Cleveland, OH 44115-2214
ISBN: 1-880834-61-8
Library of Congress Catalog
Card Number: 2003111520

The Ohio Arts Council helped fund this program with state tax dollars to encourage economic growth, educational excellence and cultural enrichment for all Ohioans.

Guide to Native Beasts

Contents

for my Cris

Sometime like apes that mow and chatter at me,
And after bite me; then like hedgehogs which
Lie tumbling in my barefoot way and mount
Their pricks at my footfall; sometime am I
All wound with adders who with cloven tongues
Do hiss me into madness.

CALIBAN

LOVE ARCHETYPE

The hedgehogs arrive nightly,
nettlesome domes roaming my brain,
treading dream's wheels.
Your tense hand shudders in the hollow of my armpit –
a hedgehog nuzzles.
Next to the toaster, a hedgehog loaf.
Hedgehog in my coat, asking
Where are you going?
Field of hedgehogs,
spines infused with horizon.
In the wild conscious world, I've seen only one
fleeing into ferns, ridiculous as a hat.
No believer in any species of sign,
I will say
Hedgehog
until they surrender their quills.

An Episode of Moose

This loneliness is nothing compared to moose.
Antlers like hands mid-clap, a body's volume,
the inexecutable bending of knees.
I have encountered moose, inconsolable
and dusty, drooping from a lodge wall
into air close with pancakes,
smoked wool, the unwashed parts of men;
zoo moose on concrete, ink-blot shadows,
austere among zebras, the anomalous apes
swinging, climbing, swinging.
I have witnessed a wake of moose penetrating water,
heads disembodied by moon;
sudden moose in dense forest
from another order of magnitude;
mother and young, fibrous, impersonating wood,
fading into lake vapors.
Stupid desolation – my empty room, dark street, silence –
I have followed a lovesick bull catapulted through birch
by a violent affinity, head fat with grief.
He mutilated the woods
with declarations of belligerent love.

CHERRIES

Because he chopped down the tree –
this story, surely a lie –
we have a symbol for honesty.
Was it in bloom, a flutter of pink,
drifting at his feet? You can see the temptation
to chop. Was it all fruit, splattering the ground,
skins slick over pits?
This waste shapes our great man.
In February classrooms, his wigged head nods
on bulletin boards; the cherries dangle,
each perfect, something to obtain.
The fruit itself is a lie:
globe of red – when you slip it through your lips,
your mouth forms the word *plump* –
inside, the flesh pales, and the stone on your tongue
like truth. You have to spit it out
while everyone watches.
A girl spreads her thighs. Her limbs quiver.
Why cherry? Why always stealing?
Disguise becomes the cherry –
syrupy pie with occasional fruit, uniformly red;
vivid bitter maraschino jewel, a nipple.
In Japan, they grow the trees for flowers;
most set no fruit. Here,
we take the sweet and sour –
our craving appetites –
and ignore the flimsy blossom.

Dowser

The forked stick dips and I ask why
does he feel the current beneath the barren
surface – why is there water waiting for him
to tell me to dig? No reason, this gift for finding
with confidence – how I envy his knowing.

The needle slips to the vein and I see
my blood escape passionless skin – barely pain,
barely a flinch – nothing to lose
except searching. I could

dial the phone – I think I could do that.
It might be worth the tones, the ringing, the click
of a line picked up, to hear
the crackle before the voice. Imminent life –

God lives in the desert deliberately.
The stunned land taken by wind – a sublimation.
No hope for something deeper – the oasis, a mirage.

It is most pure, that which leaves the surface to hide.
I will dig and drink and bathe
until the water sinks and I find
my hands pounding over a dead heart.

LOCOMOTIVE

1

The train goes nowhere, always travels
through – and the tracks leave the land
unfinished, a nation incomplete from all its
movement. We hate to see a train stopped,
filling in the blank rails.

I've never lived far from the nighttime pulse
of a train, its bovine call at empty roads –
at night, it doesn't whistle. The house,
surrounded, hums a small lament.

The rail created *place*, towns planned in empty space
with homely names of rail officials' daughters.
The engine *pushed* –
its cars merely a detail, something to trail behind.

A Chinese worker dangles in a basket, planting
charges; the cliff face shifts, embraces rails which race
to form connection. The last ten miles are laid in half a day;
a photo shows a crowd of white men – two shake hands.
A bottle of christening champagne awaits its crash. *Transcontinental* –
the bones of a thousand Chinese men return home to China.

In landscape paintings, the train enters a mouth of stumps,
a figure watches, the steam dissolves to mist,
and mist to distant clouds. The world backs into green.

2

Train bears the word *wreck*. On a train in Egypt,
someone lights a stove for tea,
and fire tears through overcrowded cars – the engine,
unaware, does not stop. The trip continues, flaming.
A man climbs out a window, jumps.
Hundreds dying thunder by. A tugboat rams
a bridge above an Alabama bayou and a train falls
into darkness festering with reptiles.

Do not say, *I dare.*
Shortcut of ties across the gully, our stride
measuring the wide air.
You cannot *touch* a train.
We put pennies on the track and dizzy ourselves
with danger. A neighbor man is found
demolished in a ditch, an aftermath.
A car of drunken classmates pauses at a crossing –
there should be a lesson;
we try to look both ways.

A rail yard worker is caught between two coupling
cars, the links push through his softness.
As long as he stays right there,
he is whole. They run to get his wife,
as if to say, *this is marriage.*

Can you say you weren't warned? Even without the clanging,
the lowering bar, the signs blinking *train* –
isn't the track always a study in perspective,
two straight lines that disappear? *Locomotive* –
why should it stop? It's crazy
to stay in one place.

3

The country mourns the train, which isn't dead.
Tourist steam trains run back and forth,
as though we could reach the past by traveling
in a simple, finite line.

In the basements of suburbia, tiny rails ring
transformed ping pong tables, and engines buzz
plastic forests, hand painted livestock;
imagination proceeds on an electric circle.

Zephyr, Empire Builder, Coast Starlight, Sunset Limited –
the restless names of romance.
Sleeping car, dining car, tunnel murmuring *into*,
obvious red caboose, the slowing towards the station.
I am running down the platform toward the porter's open door,
his *all aboard* – my luggage, an anchor. Our kiss
has made me late – the train, impatient, huffing.
I lean out my window
with the first startle of cars. You stand below me –
waving *stop*
or maybe waving *go*.

Dress

Something useless about a dress
drives my search for the perfect one,
the one that will take away my legs,
make me stand still or
arrange myself in a chair
like a pudding settling into a bowl.
A dress is a hole to slip through.
I am the food of cloth,
teeth of the zipper pulling me in,
breaking me into bust, waist, hip –
the language of dresses: dart, bias,
flare, yoke, gore –
this is not about delicacy.
The dummy inside me
keeps changing her clothes.
I hear the hangers dangling,
the metallic sound of transformation.
Men, I pity you in your obvious pants.
The perfect dress has a certain murmur –
I am the dress' painful secret,
the one everyone knows but no one mentions.

GLOVE

Beneath the glare of glass, the long black gloves await the girls
who know that glamour has fingers,
that intimacy is all about hiding.
Gloved, their arms become gesture, their hands
linger like threats at their collarbones.

There is a ritual for removal – tugging at the fingers,
hooked thumb sliding down the arm, gathering glove –
to keep others from seeing the inside.
The hand covered in skin grasps the glove,
which is suddenly exhausted.

The yellow glove gropes around the soapy sink.
The plate – a wreck settling. The glass –
disguised as water. The knife – worn dull
with washing. The spoons swirl around
the drain, measuring and measuring.

Inside of the body moves a thin latex glove
touching the organs which are otherwise untouchable,
reading the Braille of the tumor. When the surgeon
removes his gloves, he must keep washing his hands.
The electrician's heavy gloves clutch a nest of wires.

Someone's dark house – my fingerprints hide inside the glove
caressing such possessions. Protect me from thorns,
hand's bold twin, from my fist, compulsive,
tightening. Glove for my cold deeds, bland
and ceremonious. Glove to throw down; see here –

SANDWICH

When I lie in bed, I am a sandwich –
the mattress, the sheet, the meat of me,
the sheet, the blanket, the hungry air.
Noon looms on the nightstand between two sixes.
My day will consume me in bites. Here is the
comfort of layers. The inside is always the tenderest.
My heart is a tomato, all pulp and chambers.
It is much cooler between the slices.
The sandwich can only take a certain amount of pressure.
It slips into pieces under squeezing. It absorbs
all of the jelly. The man pacing the sidewalk
is pressed between two signboards reading Strike.
His attitude is of strata. He earns
minimum wage, whereas the 4th Earl
of Sandwich used his position corruptly. In 1762,
he spent twenty-four hours gaming,
eating only bread with cold meat.
His islands are our Hawaii.
His food is our food – the Reuben, the Philly cheese steak,
the club, the submarine, the poor boy, the hero.
This meal breaks my day in two –
the waxed paper folded into a package,
the symmetry of good bread.

Bats

I want them badly,
their erratic swooping, their wings finding the air's whistling
resistance. Their silhouettes absorb them,
slips of night falling
from the holes stars leave in sky.
I want their featureless dark.

All day, they hang themselves,
a soft penance. I could gather them,
each a fruit ripe with syrupy sin.
Have you ever held a bat? I
killed one once. People are always asking me
to finish things off – mice squeaking in traps,
a cat-gnawed bird. No one wants to do
what might be right. The bat, awake
and grasping in the light, ill, made us feel
unlucky. A dustpan
works well – the bat still beneath my smack.

Now outside we've hung a house to lure them in,
and yet they never come; they sense *my* sin,
my blight of good intentions.
Who am I to make decisions in the day?
What am I to night?

THE FIFTH OF JULY

The sidewalks wear mascara,
and dogs emerge from basements
to sniff the fading sausage from the air.
No one eats breakfast, the refrigerator,
all beans and pickles and condiments.
Red sticks of bottle rockets irritate the roofs.
Children wake from dreams of flying like tissues
over grass. They wander out to play with fire.
Firecracker wrappers drift like litter –
though not litter, but remnants
of the happiness of combustion.
Cardboard wheels and tiers made far away
from this place of picnic tables – the word China
means Careful, this might blow up.
Everyone knows someone who didn't let go,
who thought to tempt the fuse.
The Fourth is flags and fire trucks,
candy flung by lesser politicians,
the feet of clowns,
the taste of vinegar and salt and meat.
But today we are no longer rebels,
and there is only the calm
of having nothing to explode.

THANKSGIVING

We had traced our hands and added pitchfork feet,
flourished the scrawl with autumn-colored crayons,
so when the tom appeared in Mrs. Dalton's first grade
with his bird head bald and turning nervous blue,
as unthumblike as his drooped
wattle, hinting at a sexuality
of which we knew nothing true,
we learned the suspiciousness of birds as symbols.
The tom's noise was a hunger we tamed
by saying Gobble.

One Thanksgiving, the sink stopped up and we washed the bird
in the bathtub, rubbing under its wings
as it sat beneath the stream of water like an absentminded child.

Turkeys in the wild seem penitent, wanderers
lost in their dark ugliness, rightful emblems
of this land. Driving down an obscure wooded road,
I saw a shrink-wrapped frozen turkey in the ditch.
Was it even missed in this plenty?

Each year the President pardons a bird, purportedly in honor of Lincoln
letting his son's pet live – a moment which foretold
of all our innocent waste, our token kindnesses
and cruelties – this pardon a kind of anti-crucifixion:
one bird saved so all the others can be eaten with ceremony,
with sacredness. At a Virginia petting zoo, the pardoned bird
grows tough among the hands of children.

The Feed Store

You come here to make something yours –
the crates of chicks, soft and doubtful,
hopping beneath heat lamps – a few, still,
but breathing, weak-necked; the ducklings sweet with
quivering – for $1.75 you can bring one home in a paper bag,
grow a loaf of feathers; the striped fuzz turkey, pheasant,
quail like walnuts, goslings shoving goslings –
where does it begin, the riddle of origin? *Take one.*
Reach in with *your* hand. See
the rabbits lying limp in wire cages.

Start with the dirt itself, an end and a beginning.
Or call it *soil, earth,* if you have to.
Choose from the wall full of blades –
the dirt needs convincing.
Then the roots in buckets – potato, onion – the seeds
clicking in envelopes. The fifty-pound bags of fertilizer,
the pipes, the valves, the spigots to coax water onto seedlings.

A farm pulls its land in closer,
the pattern of green, the returning cows swinging with milk,
the fateful pig. What *follows?* What does it require?
An animal tattoo kit, a bag of plastic numbers for ears,
shoat rings, hog rings – $4.99 to lead a bull by his nose –
an electric prod – to *own* –
electric fencing, devices for opening and closing gates.
Foot rot shears, bottles of antibiotics, medicine
for dry cow, chemicals to dust the animal yard,
traps and yellow boxes of poisons –
to balance death with life.
On the shelf below the weaning masks, the leads in various lengths –
a calf nipple large as a thumb –
everything gentled with sucking.

Certainly the feed itself has duties– medicated starter, maintenance,
for flight, for laying, for fattening up –
for *feeding*. Why else are you here?

For the distractions? The silver belt buckles,
the ornamental windmill? A man scrapes his boots,
steps through the cow-belled door
into the salty odor of leather, the risen sour of grain.
He moves his hand to his hat.
You know him – he lives out on the so-and-so place –
his place, and with his gray hair, he is still
somebody's boy's youngest boy. What can you *raise*,
what *property*? Even your hatchling hen
holds every egg she'll ever lay.

Hay, Straw

I'm always asking for a bale of hay
when really I'd like a bale of straw –
the problem of tongue's habit.
Hay is for eating; straw is not,
a purposeful difference,
but I don't eat hay,
not yet, anyway.
They sell both down the road,
blocks of green or gold bound in wire.
It's like that here –
you can get what you ask for,
even if it's not what you mean to want.

TICK

The shock of simile – *full as a*
tick – and I'm shuddering, seeing the pale body,
a round, taut seed; legs foreshortened, twitching useless;
head, slipped under skin –
this *sensation*, language making it worse. I tell myself
the tick sees nothing – simply responds
to the chemicals of me, and lets go of its place
for another – no choosing, no thirst.
The tick's world is small – climb, fall, suck –
the unintricate luck of landing.
Don't be frightened.
But I wear a scar, a chainless charm on my chest,
where a tick fed one afternoon, and in fallen night,
I felt it there, finally. The lighting of a match –
flame urging it out – *enough.*
My *dread* – and yet I should be only bothered,
like the poor dog, beaded in ticks which pop as we pull;
I too am full of the blood of others,
and I never know when to stop.

LAWN SHRINES: BATHTUB VIRGINS

The more I see, the more I believe
domesticity is a sacred mystery. There she is again,
her resin skin, her blue robes pooling over her toes,
her open hands like fins at her side;
she stands in the upended claw foot tub, its drain hole sunken in
        the lawn.
Many have lain naked in her niche,
rubbing their intimate, pedestrian filth. The dirt here
is fertile. Beyond the yard, the house, the barn,
are miles of plants with roots.
I'm not a virgin
or a mother. All afternoon I drive the grid
of corn and oats, alfalfa and soy, cow and ubiquitous chicken.
I point each out in some agrarian litany.
I live in a city. Milk jug, egg carton –
these things show up on the shelves of stores.
In the winter, everyone brings their mother of God inside
and leaves the tubs out catching drifts of snow.
Even in spring, I can't really say where life comes from.

Swarm

Inexplicable bees in my tree –
inextricable – you will not leave me,
though the extension service agent tried,
with her shears and boxes, her impenetrable veil.

Please, I didn't call her; the neighbors did, their dog,
allergic, turns lumpy and listless – a Labrador retriever,
golden.

You appeared, gothic condensation of abdomens,
and I eased my hand into you, a mitten,
felt your mechanical breeze. Stay.
In illustrations, an antique catcher's vest
represents the hive.

There's a house with a hive between floor and ceiling.
The room weeps honey, a domestic miracle.
The family recovers from ecstasy, screws a jar
to the ceiling, enjoys toast and glazed ham.
I have plenty of flowers.

Bees dance,
and this may or may not help them find nectar;
they pace in loops, insect Shakers
twitching with devotion.
I convert. I waggle –

but you rise from your branch, sublime,
a sound collapsing
into the lawns and shrubs,
and I cannot keep you.

Emus

I imagine they have value, these poultry
populating the filbert farm-lined roads,
as possible as cows. A group gathers
near an aluminum shed, heads wobbling
like unattended nozzles; their bodies undulate,
tip gymnastically in dust clouds.
They have traded flight
for feathers. I predict disaster.
I've heard you can eat them,
use their eggs for decorations,
but here they loiter, bulging, tasteful
and tame as plastic deer.
Somewhere – not here, where we are slow with reason
and recklessness –
their former breeders have released them.
All supply and no demand; most people have enough
foolishness. An exodus of emus,
embellishing the wild.
A drove of necks. They have been known to attack
and run – as I imagine I will
when faced with the fact
that I am both unholy and useless.

THE AUCTION

Someone told him *Get rid of it all* –
with his flurrying words and numbers,
his throat echoing, and we are pulled in,
blinking at voice and its permutation –
   twenty, twenty suddenly *twenty-five, thirty* –
and we make this happen somehow,
our tipping chins, our lifted fingers.
So we sit rigid, not wanting to end up with
   a nice mashed potato bowl, dirty – needs a bath;
   railroad lantern, glass missing;
   everything in the box, everything – five, five,
   five dollar bill out there?
We know these things,
have browsed through the tables on the lawn,
picking up whatnot, putting it down,
all control, all silence before loss. We like
a choosing, a delay – but here he is calling
desire to desire, a panic of possessiveness –
Yours, you say? Well –
the competition of want, the wrestle.
Yet when he slams the gavel, writes down our number,
then the shame of taking. *Going* –
the sewing machine, the truck, the rug,
the depression glass dish with its perpetual fade.
I have had nothing to say for days –

but someone is giving it all up.
Backs of overalls shift in lawn chairs,
wind on the microphone, yellow jackets in the grass,
the illusory itch of gain, of pleasure in sound. The highest bidder
  nods.
We are going; we are gone.

The truth is, that a Pigmy and a Patagonian, a Mouse and a Mammoth, derive their dimensions from the same nutritive juices. The difference of increment depends on circumstances unsearchable to beings with our capacities. Every race of animals seems to have received from their Maker certain laws of extension at the time of their formation. Their elaborative organs were formed to produce this, while proper obstacles were opposed to its further progress. Below these limits they cannot fall, nor rise above them. What intermediate station they shall take may depend on soil, on climate, on food, on a careful choice of breeders. But all the manna of heaven would never raise the Mouse to the bulk of the Mammoth.

Thomas Jefferson,
Notes on the State of Virginia

Giant Fiberglass Cow

Cow,
your brown wears thin from midnight rides
of teenage rodeo wanna-bes.
Your side bears brands from cigarettes.
Your blue eyes fade to dreamy white;
you stand like a sleep walker in the parking lot,
unwitting prop of the cheese gift shop.
Small things gravitate towards large.

Now the interstate sleeks through town
and hauls along a fast food joint,
smearing the sky with its margarine mmm –
You glow; the headlights churn around, around.
You bow, a harmless beast
accumulating grime and trust,
harboring a pastoral conspiracy.

I know I'm not the only one to lie beneath
the moon of your udder
and drink the milk-beams streaming down
and strain to hear the wisdom of your lowing.
The city grows.
So when you go, don't leave me here,
unweaned,
too slow with cream to follow.

The tree across the field flutters with black leaves at sunrise,
a breeze emptying the branches, leaves in spirals in the nomenclature
of fall. Then, contrary, the leaves lift, return, trimming the tree and I
      hear it,
a crowd of irritated children and see the leaves are starlings,
hundreds, sudden and migrainous, like hatred.
Sturnus vulgaris – the birds are foreigners and I, their xenophobe,
cursing Eugene Scheiffelin who, in 1890, released a flock in New York
      City,
wanting all the world of birds to be a copy of Shakespeare's England.
Speckled, speaking in tongues, they screech at morning's goodness
and mimic the work of the season, its simple loss.
Someone, too, brought me here – I know – imposter.
My neighbor wants to chop down the tree –

he's offered me the wood. Would I want
such a thing in my fire – that leaps so easily between death and life?

Boy with Imaginary Baseball

He's in the street again, swinging
his bat between the rows of parked cars,
windshields taut and snug, holding in their radios.
His hips twist inside his pants,
the bat, extended, pulling against his grip
like the weight of a dancer; he could
let it go –
but he sees the ball, suddenly close, its spin,
familiar. Behind the doors of houses,
people eat hot dogs.
It touches the sweet spot of the bat
where his small strength murmurs through the wood.
Up and down the street, envelopes in mailboxes.
He sends it rising into the trees. Leaves hog the sun.
The world dissolves into bases.
He runs, the air crowding his lungs to cheer,
his head, all teeth and tongues.

Horse Girl

In a classroom of two-legged children,
she is sketching a horse on the back of the lesson.
She knows the hard curves that make up the body –
the haunch, the hinge of the jaw –
knows which way the joints bend, the puzzle
of muscle and hooves. The horse isn't standing
plagiaristically still, a diagram marked *withers*, *fetlock*;
it twists under her hand with a laming insistence.

She knows something is missing and calls it Horse.
At home, the plastic horses wait tamely on her shelf,
named and thoroughbred. When she arranges them,
she lifts each as though she's answering a telephone.

Horses remind me of art supplies.
Or else, they're tanks of hay and gas and steam
standing mudshorn at the fence, tongues working against bits.
They're a pair of tails wiping the back of a trailer.
When a horse slips to the ground in battle, the rider
crouches behind it and rests his rifle on its ribs.

Her horse is a ticket.
It grows against her erasings; it is ready to go.
Around her, children watch chalk glide over the green board
and race to raise their hands. They wish for gerbils in cages
with wheels and tubes,
the preciousness of small.
She will leave them behind –
their flat faces, soft and terrible.

HANDS

The man with the deformed hands
cannot clap.
He pounds his foot instead; the floor applauds.
When he meets you, he nods politely, alone in
his shaking. See where he puts
his fists, the roots of worry, vegetable
unloveliness – he will show you
how to hold a thing. The lock
invites his key, snugly turning. A fallen sequin
teases him on the rug. And you,
in your shameful gloves, imprisoned
by your rings, your lacquered fingernails –

this world is an affliction of cuffs. He would
climb blouses – unbuttoning, unbuttoning, unbuttoning, unbuttoning.

At the Costume Shop

People search for the perfect wound,
the deformity to match
the black cloak they will pull around themselves
as they step from night into someone's lit living room
where they will be recognized, finally.
Overweight children try on the skins of cats.
There aren't enough monsters to meet demand.
Bland teen clerks with blue dyed hair, glued on mustaches, fake tattoos,
tell the crowd to grab a number, stand in line –
Listen, they whisper, we're experts.

I used to anticipate the handing down of costumes,
a surety to it, like going through a phase. I knew someday
I'd be the hobo, the pioneer girl, the dirndled German –
always something to grow into.

Now, at the house of two women who are also lovers,
I stand in a den that was once a garage
with a police officer, a surfer, a punk rocker
(is this much of a fantasy?)
watching men wearing football uniforms
play football on television.
Nuts fill bowls on the table. A friend in lederhosen
crosses his legs, talks of news and work.
My smile wears off on a plastic cup.

Sad, sad candy in wrappers, in dishes in vestibules.
Sad temporary sweetness. I am what I want to be –
I'm just not convincing. You
who see some other you – one who will surprise everyone,
one who deserves rewards –
when you come to my door,
I'll give you handfuls.

The Taxidermist's Mother

The taxidermist's mother
pays homage to her son's art
each holiday season. Eight stuffed deer
stand bridled with lights and bells in trampled snow.
One lowers its head, antlers like exposed roots
of a fallen tree. Another lifts a hoof
testing the air for dubious gravity. Nothing
gets off the ground in this town.
A plywood Santa tempts the icy roof,
dragging his bag of anonymous toys.
Parents prop their children against the deer,
a festive grotesque. Across the street, a plastic snowman glows
with incandescent indigestion. The traffic migrates
as the taxidermist's mother reassures passers-by:
these deer were donated by the highway department.
Behind her picture window with painted frost,
a Canada goose lands in perpetuity. No one
should care that deer aren't reindeer
and that reindeer can't fly. Headlights sweep the yard.
The shadows jump like a reflex surfacing through skin.

Zamboni Man, The Mall

After the frosting girls, beautiful
and bitter with color, blade us dizzy;
after the music winds them up
and lets them go –
and we are left lumpish at our railings,
aware, suddenly, of our legs in pants,
of our grasp on packages of towels and bras
and unremarkable socks;
after we have lost our hopes
to the grief of immeasurable commonness,
he appears. He wears a white shirt.
His machine, a mystery,
scrapes and drips, rids the surface
of grace – all traces of ecstasy
replaced with ice. We depend on his vindication,
his promise to make everything clear again.
Somewhere skaters untie their laces.

Christmas – the season for death by fire –
all warm things the flip side of tragedy –
the hearth, the stove, the string of lights
sparking. The candle – touching the tissue wrapping in her hand,
then the drapes, then – she cannot stop a thing
that wants so extravagantly. Or – needles smoldering,
almost silent. I saw the smoke,
the black stairwell, the paneless windows, the water from the hoses
frozen in blasts – this story. A holiday matinee
at the Iroquois Theater – the curtain ignites,
and the orchestra plays while the crowd leaps. We cannot stop
ourselves from shoving at locked doors. What about
Him, delivered from the flames? The bright star
leading to a savior lying in a manager
in a stable snug with beasts? So we believe in calm escape,
our divine *proof* – not our well-proven
subjection, our mundane tendency to burn.

Epitaph

In these winter days
when broken corn stalks protrude
from the fields' snow skin,
I think of you, Leonard J. Rudzinski,
your sixty-three-year-old body
slipping deeper into the silo
as you tried to swim the quicksand pull
of 30,000 pounds of corn
escaping from a chute below.
Did you feel betrayed by the fickle grain
which kept you living so many seasons
only to turn, kernels at your face,
the corrugated steel bin
swallowing you whole?
Did your drowning man's struggle
dig your grave of corn?
Or did you, delirious with corn dust,
recall the sweet sour green of the field in August,
the silver fountains of silk between your fingers,
and give in to the collapsing corn above,
plunge closer to the opening
where hours later rescuers delivered your body,
bruise blue, stillborn?

Holly Hobby Dolls

They fill the toy store ads
like mail-order brides.
I have two –
one, big as a baby,
the other, travel size.
They wear dresses of pre-printed patchwork.
Yarn braids hang from blue sunbonnets
glued to their cotton skulls.
Underneath, their heads are bald,
bodies, bland,
figures, flattened by naptime weight.
They purse their painted lips in unison,
pillow features reflecting a twin placidity.

I pretend I'm Laura Ingalls' blind sister, Mary,
beat furniture with a stick, feel my way across the house.
Bored, I'm reduced
to crawling, eyes closed, up the stairs,
lying on the landing
listening to my sister read in her room.
Her fingers separate the pages.
She breathes, bedsprings shift.
She has all the Little House on the Prairie books
with custard-colored spines lined up like teeth along the bookshelf.
I tell her I have scarlet fever,
press my palms against her face.
This is how I see.

For the Bicentennial
our mother sews us matching calico costumes.
Outside, wild beasts howl and pace the sidewalk.
For Christmas I want a dog that bites.

Vera's: Hunter, Kansas

A child, I knew a woman owned the place and imagined
what I could of sin, saw in my dim mind
a torch singer, her curves in thin silk,
hair languid in the smoke, nails like glass,
her voice low and choking.
I had never been anywhere – had only visited.

In so many places, there is nothing left
but history and taverns. In this town,
my father's high school sits abandoned.
The basement gym fills up with water.
The building is stone and stuck. Somewhere inside,
boys with ducktails smack each other with towels,
lean on the wooden stairs
practicing their scowls and smirks to show some outside world.

Vera's giant car is clean and parked
out front. The license plate reads VERA.
I'm old enough to drink and hold my tongue.
She's at the bar, her face a sunken gourd, her hair,
sweepings of dust, vast breasts inside her t-shirt.
She's been open for decades.

Two college boys play pool; it's summer and they're wasting time
pretending they're not long gone, would never leave.
They egg her on to sing with lust "On the Wings of a Dove,"
the jukebox loud, the sound, no place to go.
In posters on the walls, women wearing only thongs and heels
wrap their thighs around barstools
and look up smiling from their beer.

REUNION

Young, you smile.
Your uniform smiles.
Your young wife's collarbones smile.
Your mother and father, smiling, smiling.
Your grandmother smiling,
her teeth widowing her gums.

Uncle Walter unsnaps his overall straps,
flap in his lap like a tongue.
Your hand on his chest,
his pacemaker grinds,
a gizzard
full of gravel.

They find your brother in the wheat field,
wrapped in an unusual chill,
enchanted,
beard sugared with breath.
His body thaws, dough
on the kitchen table.

Your father's bones infect his blood.
He sits, a stone post by the stove.
He wears a grey and painful suit
and strokes the handle of his cane.
He holds a pill between his lips,
waiting for a sip of water.

Your breast clenches
its garlic fist.
Your veins are everywhere.
Your wife shakes your wrist like a rubber glove.
Your pulse resurfaces,

thick as sausage.

Your fevered son runs sobbing down the stairs -
he thinks he's thrown you in the laundry chute.
He cradles a pair of underwear.
Limp, he surrenders to bed,
delirious
as the last dodo.

WIDOWED

She plants only yams -
a good year for yams.
Ear wax of the earth.
Plugging the ground,

he sweats in his box.
His silver tie cleaves his ribs.
Lapels fin.
His jugs of water on the stairs are gone.

Fifty years, the house never burned.
The stairs gestated a needless fear.
She threw out all the jugs.
Thirsty stairs.

Upstairs, the bathtub spigot
drools, russeting
the enamel shell.
Amphibious,

her teeth swim in their glass.
Downstairs, the piano, hammers suspended on strings.
Slipcovered chairs hold imprints of guests
beneath a wall of photograph skins.

Energy crackles under the rugs.
Onions suffocate in drawers.
Eyes sprout.
The stove,

burnt lobes flowing out of
the pot. The root, its molasses robe
slipping over her gums, she anticipates.   She
anticipates.

He who believes in the struggle for existence and in the principle of natural selection, will acknowledge that every organic being is constantly endeavoring to increase in numbers; and that if any one being varies ever so little, either in habits or structure, and thus gains an advantage over some other inhabitant of the same country, it will seize on the place of that inhabitant, however different that may be from its own place.

Charles Darwin,
The Origin of Species

Chicken

At 63rd Street's Harold's Chicken Shack
the neon chicken turns her back
on an axe-wielding pursuer,
her flightless flight, the flapping gas in tubes.
She eludes the blue slice,
squawks electric.
Behind bulletproof glass, a woman
basks in the soothing haze of dinners.
Wings pop in baskets.
She spins a bucket of livers
through the revolving window.
Outside, beneath the elevated tracks,
she's seen men's bodies spill.

The argon lights trudge far beyond
the city's heart of slaughteryards,
now closed. Consider all the parts
of things – the living, the machines. The chicken,
its two halves upon a nest
of fries, blanketed with bread to sponge
the paper plate, the plastic knife
to separate the leg from thigh.
The woman's drawer
with bills in slots. The train,
its parallel rails. The egg's still shell.

Hammer

You hold the tool of doing
and undoing. The weight of the head
fighting your wrist, drawing itself toward
pound, the handle's grain ringing. Two fingers
steady the nail, then the gentle tap
preceding the blow. How can the nail
stand it, this swift betrayal?
The hammer is the soul of change.
The pictures float on the wall,
the roof crouches overhead –
can things really stay like this?
The forked claw slips against the wood,
the satisfying squeak of lost resistance.
I am the stuck nail bending.
All morning, the sound of distant hammers –
I am so tired,
I lay my head on the table like a watermelon.
A man carries nails between his lips,
as though explaining a plan.
The nail steals the hammer's act –
we say Christ was nailed to the cross,
but he was the carpenter's boy;
they hammered him there.

It's true that regret abides, but what of it?
A story needs loss, and we've all heard of the birds'
endless flock passing over, perpetual as seconds replacing
seconds – what were a few wasted? But then,
wasn't there an end, closing the tidy lesson?
A fourteen-year-old boy, the cusp of man, his sins
all curiosity, all blouses and stolen sweets, all furtive
curses, all doubts in God, all simple blood –
he sees a strange bird in the barnyard and asks his mother –
yes, a *boy* – for the shotgun. Innocent –
only wanting to study a still thing in death.
A local woman stuffs the bird, sews shoe buttons on for eyes –
it takes years for someone to say for certain *last*.

There are more unprecedented crimes than his; we lose
our boy to a man's designful guilts, yet even in old age
he tells of the cold morning, and the bird stops eating corn,
flaps into its tree, waiting for the boy to return with the gun –
and *there* the bird endures – and behind glass, "Buttons,"
artlessly preserved, a clumsy denouement dragging out
extinction like a sky of dark wings, like slow forgiveness.

SPONTANEOUS GENERATION

This was good science – the mud,
cold womb for life. The non-living
bearing the small creatures.
See the meat, how it transforms to curls of maggots,
the grain composes furred bodies of mice.
The world was more hopeful back then,
mere stuff, the ingredients for being.
A rag, a dark corner, a piece of cheese,
a spot of still water littered with leaves –
I have these things around,
but I know *ex ovo omnia* –
everything comes from the egg.
What were those great thinkers thinking,
before Pasteur proved that pure air is barren,
that only the living cause the living?
And yet, the sudden shadowy cockroach,
the silverfish appearing like dust –
we are all capable of misconceptions
and terrible conceptions.
You too have wished
to make a life out of nothing.

ROAD

The deer's posture speaks
the meticulous language of disaster.
Any attempt to resuscitate would be only

yawns
inadequate
against the impenetrable atmosphere

of breathlessness.
A tourist,
I turn automatically,

maintain polite
distance,
proper conduct

when encountering
poverty.
Am I not an authentic pilgrim,

guardian of vision,
worn by excess of travel?
My travel is recreation.

One deer
is not chaos
compromising my skin.

Wool

Our local winner of the Make It Yourself With Wool
contest will travel to Reno this summer
for the national competition.
Her winning floral pantsuit
flusters around her hips.
Petunias erupt,

spread.
She has never been to Reno.
Will she be too warm
in Reno
in the summer
in her pantsuit?

Sheared sheep emerge
translucent as opals,
only a thin membrane
keeping the colors
in.
If sheep see light

through a knothole in their crib,
they believe
they can fit through the hole.
They will butt themselves unconscious trying
to fit through
the hole.

Remember to fill holes with available opaque material.
An old shirt. A
dishrag.
A man kept sheep tied to stakes
around his lawn.
They ate circles

of grass
down to dirt.
Sheep have been known to taste
and swallow
nails.
Infection blossoms

invisible
in their punctured gut.
Some sheep break their legs running downhill.
You might find them bleating
in their crumpled, curly foam.
Lambs led to slaughter

leap.
Their panic,
ejective.
I have seen whole ramps of them
jumping
higher than any man.

LUNAR ECLIPSE: HALE-BOPP OVER PALO ALTO

We are not surprised to see the moon decay
into night. It is time for dinner;
the oven cycles, a release of heat.

In the garden, costume jewelry snails ravish the delphiniums.
Over the street, a star rubs the sky,
evidently a smudge.

Methodical, the washing machines cannot escape their dials.
The blonde man and woman wear only white
beneath their trench coats. (I have seen them before,
staring across a donut.)
Acrobat pants in the dryers –
a college boy folds a basket of sweatshirts,
his underwear in squares.

Underneath his trench coat, the man removes his clothes.
Underneath her trench coat, the woman removes her clothes,
trench coat arms gesturing listlessly
as she slips off her blouse.

Then, the insertion of quarters, the drum
fills with water. The man and woman know exactly
what happens to their clothes.

Off Sand Hill Road, the venture capitalists start their cars
and park their cars.
A man walks up the road and down the road,
always walking on this road, always this adventure.
When he leaves his orbit, he will walk into the crack
where the earth shifts, where damage is usually irreparable.

TORNADO

We have practiced crouching for disaster –
the siren echoing down an empty hall –
ready for a kind of surgery.
The sky leaves the land behind, furiously still –
wind and water hollow on roofs.
It is most dark

when we close our eyes.
Schoolchildren in balls on the locker room floor,
their noses near the salty tiles, necks tucked,
arms covering ears, hands clasped on backs of heads,
holding everything together; they believe they will be saved
by following directions. The storm builds

with our waiting. We huddle by the water heater, the basement green,
our father, on the porch, not quite ready to retreat,
our steady pleading. Close by, a classmate's horse
is lifted gently into air, set gently back.
I wouldn't call this weather

this decisiveness. A man steps outside, sees
his neighbor's house gone, his clothesline still dripping
with shirts. A child wakes to find himself abandoned
by his ceiling.
I can explain how it works:
instability, rotation, wind, moisture,
front, thunder, vortex, supercell, downdraft, luck,
surprise, pressure, collapse,

rotation, wind. Fastidious chance.
A couple sits on the sofa watching the cloud grasp the ground
when their picture window implodes.
Their bodies are crystalline with shards.
A boy crawls from a ditch, his ears deaf with dirt.

Irrelevant boundaries – this is communion,
not collision. The confetti of feathers

in wind. Storm implies something angry,
not absurd. Everyone agrees that it sounds like a freight train –
A freight train, they say, over and over.
They should have seen it coming.
One man offers, A squadron of jets.
The siren sounds

the town into hiding, yet a man gets into his truck.
His wife holds the video camera. When the funnel touches down,
ripping through phone lines, they cannot believe their luck.
They race along, recording, the rush of winding tape.
The land awaits its erasing.

In the thunder of night, the hum of the fan stops,
and the room is all lightning and humid portent.

Like any revolution, there is debris.
Follow the carcasses of machinery, cement blocks, snapped trees,
the inside things suddenly out – a bill with an address,
a table leg, a cloud of insulation,
the churned and crumpled beasts, still as toys.
When things stop falling,
that means it is over.

CADAVER

If one knows the muscles on a cat, the transition to
man is easy – his corpse transforms to chart,
and we see matter for matter, unlayering
like suspicion –
trapezius, serratus ventralis, external oblique –
etymology of *body*, each meaning
to move. He was fifty-five, obese, a smoker,
and now, for what he is, he is old;
we rub him softer with petroleum jelly, but nothing replaces
the fluency of blood. We resist his passivity –
give up the chambers of your heart,
give up your hidden spleen.
The sinews of man make nothing simple.
The faint feel their heads
above their familiar spines.

We fold him back together, zip him into his bag.
Around us, shelves hold secrets in jars – glassy
fetal horse, a palmful of unborn pigs –
did we need to know this? *To fall, to fall –*
cadaver, you've made mistakes,
forgive us all.

LOSS OF CONFIDENCE AT THE LAST SECOND

Always the precipice,
the difference between dangle
and drop. I would like to say I'm ready for knuckles to reverberate
    my door,
for the damp hand of opportunity to grab my hand,
flapping my elbow like a flag.
But then what? I'm expected to pick up the ringing phone?
Today is cloudy and my neighbors are losing their roof.
I hear it falling, a rhythmic exposure,
the house letting out its held breath,
rooms filling with sky.
Who made this decision?
I'll be keeping my furniture indoors.
Why did I want to step off the porch,
cross the street with its undoubtable traffic?
How could the chorus of brakes
be more lovely than I imagine?

Sonnet

I have my own butcher.
He knows what cuts I'd like – my various chops,
my tongue laid out for wrapping – I could take and take.
Today he has before him an opened beast
and a perfectly normal saw, his table great
with meat, his blade moving between the blades of bone,
straightening the confusion of tendons and fat, measuring the
        pounds in his red hand.
Oh, for the seasonings and the fire, for my own sharp knife,
my fork to pin it down and lead it to my mouth.
He manipulates a loin into a steak and lets me watch, feeds
        sausage into casings –
everything gives, except hunger, resurrected over and over, intact.
I am falling into pieces, swathed in paper –

some are frozen, buried deep in lockers;
some are ready to eat.

Air Show: F-16s above Cleveland

Clearly, we are part of the performance, slowing our
cars on the freeway, errands interrupted
like dull dreams of waking, taking a shower,
interrupted by the true alarm. The solo jets
low above, turning into some trick, some loop or roll
we can't see through the towers of downtown –
just the roar chasing the flash of plane,
catching it overhead. Then the diamond of jets
needling through smokestacks, wing to wing, using principles of trust
I don't understand, but I understand this –
not *pilot* or *engine* or *maneuver* –
the trick here is panic, and I play along – Dear whomever:

spare this city, slow to recover, our hazy old sky.
Spare our lives awaiting attack. Spare our somnambulant cars.

THE DOG AGE

The dog learns to chase its tail.
It dervishes
the linoleum.
It rotates on an axis
of attention.
Its loyalty,
centrifugal,
separating into dog
and water.
It drinks.

The dog orbits on command,
sheds electrons,
splits
into chasing head,
fleeing tail.
We are all
at risk.
This is the revolution.

The dog learns to dig.
Dig, dig, dig, dig,
dig, dig, dig.

Externalities dissatisfy the dog.
Sensing burial,
it scoops.
Nothing escapes exhumation by the vigorous dog.

The dog debones the dirt.
Now we may consume the meat.

The dog learns to speak.
Requests biscuit.

Warns of imminent elimination.

The dog says
Ham. Enter ham in dish.
The dog says
Squirrel. Plump squirrels plummet from trees.
The dog says

Sock, shoe. We walk
unadorned, scornful furlessness
of toe exposed, feet stripped of kick.

No apology from dog. No please.
No need for translation.

Again and again, an infestation – because the world disapproves
of emptiness – the rats dragging bones and nuts into holes in the garden,
a network of detritus, buried as desire; the mice
scratching, squealing in the walls like ghosts of arguments; the slugs
finding night quiet with blossoms –
oh, I took care of them all. My grim schemes.

But for days it's been flying ants, the air filled with an invasive sparkle.
They land tingling on me, drown in my glass.
There's not much to each body to hate – a speck, a nerve, a mechanism
        to fly –
wings barely – more the lightness of arcane purpose. Then dumb death –
the sink, the screen, the lamp, the puddle of water, my brushing hand –
they made it just this far. I worry

that I should be more worried – the harm lies
somewhere unreachable, and I delicately succumb.

You'll be interested to know that the Italian navigator has just landed in the new world.

> Arthur Holly Compton,
> *coded message to James Bryant Conant after
> Enrico Fermi's first controlled self-sustaining
> nuclear reaction, December 2, 1942*

Were the natives friendly?

> James Bryant Conant,
> *in reply*

From a Steam Engine Manual

Engines interrupt
bone, erode the uniform hand.
Fingers easily reject knuckles.
Avoid urges of any kind when inspecting pistons.
Before inserting a remedial crowbar
into belts or chains,
remember that the engine is a
reciprocating engine.

Clean boiler tubes daily.
Tumult thrives in captivity and
threatens containers.
Never stir coals with prostheses;
fire does not distinguish
between real fuel and false
limbs. After releasing steam,
check ground for hot birds.

Wheels reduce stationary man
to soil.
Avoid lounging.
The path of progress is paved
with half moons of abandoned toes.

The spirit of the living creatures was in the wheels

I'm trying to draw a perfect circle –
my pen anticipates diameter, the invisible spoke
of radius shifting like prophesy, stirring the page –
my soup of trials. Round is always easy, but
I don't want an egg, an excited ball, a nefarious hole,
a bomb with a short fuse – BAM! The world – without a model.

I could drop a smooth stone down the well
but the light would reflect my face and, actually,
the well is dry. A square – look everywhere –
the crystalline salt of my dried tears of frustration.
My head bears the circle, its nimbus;
my hand – the straying disciple.

With a circle, there is no stopping –
I must start over.

HERB MORRISON REPORTING ON THE HINDENBURG, MAY 6, 1937

The point was transcription – the Presto recorder with its wax disc,
its lathe and amplifier – to show his station the value
of reproduction, of an event carried away
from a time – and so he chose the Nazi airship's anniversary landing
to re-land in the future – radio's déjà entendu.
The choreography of the mooring, of journey's return;
he could describe this in words worth saving for later –
windows *like glittering jewels*, the ship riding *like some great feather*,
a *great floating palace*, majestic, simple – all evangelizing.
Then –

can we blame him for continuing to tell?
Five hundred foot flames, the frame falling – and
he calls to his engineer, *Get this Charley*, the disc
wearing under his voice's weight, *Oh the humanity!*

Though they know the news already, listeners the next morning
share his terror over toast and coffee
as the recording is broadcast – the now bland preamble
slipping effortlessly toward ruin, the witness forever surprised,
begging us to see – *Ladies and gentlemen* –
replaying like history.

Beauty Contest: Sweetheart of Hanford Engineer Works, Queen of Safety, 1944

Never mind that you don't know what you are building –
this is building *morale* – the sight of legs
on stage for the sake of your watching –
legs still, a modeled pair; legs split, walking,
converted to chase by your whistling reaction. Divide
38,500 men by 625 square miles of sand –
it's ugly, where money will bring you, what you give up.
The body above the legs turns away, all curves –
you deserve this. *Don't worry about work*; this is a war
of secrets. The torso unfolds two arms. Hands
twist on wrists, waving the plated tin cup. The land surrenders to
    concrete,
the sky to wires. Are you tired of the job's demands?
The bodies of men in barracks, the wind, the pressure of quiet?
The neck tilts – refined, pure beauty –
the hair, the silent lips, the nose,
the transfiguring crown – the *face. Don't answer anyone's questions.*
More whistles. The show is coming to a close.

BELLY

She walks it by me,
her knit top reaching unsuccessfully
for her pants –
she has never known nakedness.
Mornings, I wave weights through the air,
iron pompons, cheerful with power.
I have exposed myself to thousands of mirrors.
I lie unfolded on the floor.
Dust fills the air above me.
I snap shut like a cot;
I can sniff my knees.
Some men wear their belts above it.
Zippers high, they fumble in the washroom,
slacks like soup bowls.
Others hang it over the edge, a lamprey
feeding on resolutions.
Fifty years ago we blasted an atoll –
fifteen-megaton detonations, fallout,
coconut stands atomized, incidents of accidental exposure.
On beaches everywhere, women with nosecone breasts
showed off their navels.
Later we removed inches of topsoil,
and the natives were invited to return.

Publicity Photo, Operation Crossroads:
Mushroom Cloud Cake

I am not an atomic playboy.
   - Admiral W. H. P. Blandy

A detonation of confectioner's sugar and angel food
grows from a stretch of ordinary tablecloth
out of a bed of icing braids and pompon flowers.
The wife of Admiral W. H. P. "Spike" Blandy holds her hand
like a glove digesting bones
over the Admiral's own. She has sliced cakes before,
knows how to pull the wedge from the whole,
work a piece gently so as not to lose the tip,
leave an attractive gash. The Admiral has spoken,
or is about to speak, his mouth unclosed,
his head unstable on his neck. She was perhaps lovely
before her face became a thin box
for the display of hats.

When the picture hits the papers, priests across the country
erupt in conscientious outrage –
such mockery of apocalypse –
as if they knew nothing of celebrations
of death and miracle. Of course,
the cake is tasteless.
A week before, a patriotic baker in Illinois
sifts his flour into a bowl,
separates two dozen eggs; the yolks, two dozen suns;
the whites, whipped into peaks; the bakery air,
a fog of sweetness as something rises in the heat.

Project Chariot: Cape Thompson, Alaska, 1958

If your mountain is not in the right place, just drop us a card.
          – Edward Teller

Edward Teller, father of the H-bomb, you want to redeem your
      bad son,
to blow something up *for good*, show everyone
power's noble intentions –
and so you turn to Alaska, a place barren
of invention – *there's nothing up there.* It's a question
of what to do, not how.
We all love to play with fire, turn the wood, the burn biting away,
      the threat
of the flames escaping, watch it disappear –
the attraction of simple change. It will take just a few
thermonuclear bombs to blast 70 million cubic feet of earth
into the stratosphere. You see a harbor
form as the ocean rushes in; you see *ships carrying things* –
ignore the nine months of ice. Your hands
dredge the sand, a shallow pool to fill your mind with boats –

I want to think of you this way, to make excuses. But clearly
it's not about use – this lust to explode. You're a man
of science – you want a crater, some fallout to measure,
then the immeasurable possibility of data – *what next?* and
then what next? The chain of wonder building, regardless.

THE NAMING OF ADAM

What shall my west hurt me? As west and east
In all flat maps – and I am one – are one,
So death doth touch the resurrection.
          - John Donne, "Hymn to God, My God, in My Sickness"

The world is small, and the small of this world get smaller,
until particles have parts of particles, each its own world
with its own name – Up, Down, Charm, Strange, Bottom, Top –
as if by breaking things down, we could command it all.
Amerigo – your name made the map –
so discovery and creation share this – the origin of names –
and outlandish births lead to outlandish names –
the name, a leash to call things back
into obedience. Take Oppenheimer's Trinity –
the spirit, the flesh, the father – sacrifice and gain, or
Fat and Little, Man and Boy – pitiable and fragile –
the irony of code, the bombs dropping to their own deaths.
Later, there's Bravo, a runaway test out at sea –
Bravo! Applause rushing from the theater,
the audience, a blast of palms surfacing
from an ocean of chairs –
the cloud, an expanding ego...
try to reel it in, away from the Islanders, the bystanders,
away from the Japanese fishermen on the nearby Lucky Dragon.

Try to bring it back with that name, any name;
try to un-name it, this force –
the small worlds splitting into God.

Mutually Assured Destruction

Somewhere, someone is caressing the button – I doubt
it's a button – maybe a switch, a lever
needing force to punctuate decision. This is what scares me –
I pretend to know your name – my hand on your thigh –
but I couldn't introduce you, couldn't find your face
in a crowd of like faces – anticipatory, concerned
about the increasing pressure
of my palm, my intentions. I'm certain I have none.
Who really makes a decision? It's not
a box wrapped in decoupage, a nice flourish of paint on china. No –
a decision – who would make a thing so ugly? No one likes
outcome – only missiles whistling – danger,
a coquette, quiescent.
Your silhouette hangs on the wall, an unblemished
target. I enjoy playing with shadows; my fist –
a dog – barks. It has no teeth. Maybe
it *is* a button. You twitch
beneath my grip – Stop. Think of your poor trousers, of what
my nails could do.

Man Fishing: Point Beach Nuclear Plant, Two Creeks, Wisconsin

It takes an error to father a sin.
> – Robert Oppenheimer, in a letter to his brother, Frank

He is hoping for salmon, had seen salmon yesterday
but was carrying the wrong lures. This is called
opportunity. The reactor contains two streams, flowing
inside tubes. What happens is not confluence.
One of the streams is harmless.
The man has several rods ready against the railing.
Lake Michigan rushes into the plant
and out, slightly warmed, under his feet. Beyond,
dead alewives grease the surface. Gulls feed.
The Visitors' Center receptionist hands out complimentary calendars
full of cookie recipes. All salmon in the lake
are stocked, raised to be caught. Breeding
is doubtful. The man's skin grows painful
with sun. People carrying empty lunch coolers come out of the plant.
People carrying full lunch coolers go into the plant
to replace the people who came out –
shifts of people passing in the parking lot.
Downshore a chinook has washed up on the sand,
decaying into bone and stink. Everyone on the beach
wears shoes, the sand, incised with zebra mussel shells.
The mussels are foreign; they proliferate. They filter.
No one eats them. They plug the pipes bringing water
from the lake, each pipe a throat swallowing.
Each operator trains in an exact copy of the control room.
There were huge salmon yesterday. It's true
that everyone lies.

Canoeing the Hanford Reach

Do you trust
the canoe, its relentless wobbling, the water
pressuring it to tip? And yet you are drawn to lean
over, watch your paddle divide the wet sky,
the river split the land – and *you helping*, slipping
down the center like a secret
carried into the heart,
trying not to splash.

We all learn to right capsized canoes where I come from;
we know the drill –
swim underneath, grasp the frame, and flip – imbalance
won't surprise us – only the thrill of calamity.
The canoe is built on doubt –
it gives us a chance to be rescued.

Do you rest assured? Still, the shallow edge is best –
the salmon beneath your feet, hinting
at *the surface*. The middle
moves more swiftly, shapeless as
an unused mirror. Your paddle prods the murk,
the current's *verge* – give in.
At least when you scrape bottom,
you know you can get out.

TRACTOR

Somewhere you have a tractor.
A man finds his father's tractor
in someone else's barn, someone else's county.
When he last saw it, no one had
air conditioning. He cannot remember the names
of the dogs of boyhood –
but the machine, the relic of tinkering,
he knows, has watched his shadows
pass under it. Power is what happens when
ego has nowhere to go. Imagine
the tractor. It is cresting a bulge
of dirt, the mesmerized tires,
the lathering stack. It turns, tips, no shift
in weight, only weight itself
pulling, a kind of destiny.
A boy carries his arm across acres,
the approaching house, empty, the arm's bones and tears,
the juggle at the door.
He climbs into the bathtub
so he won't bleed on his mother's floors.
The tractor leaves a testament of pull.
Men return to the field,
triggering the clutch with a broom handle, hips
lonely for knees;
the slopes roll up around them.
No machine I could kill you with
would be this heavy.

Abandoned House Near Hanford Nuclear Reservation

Years ago, someone expected this house to be here at the end of
    the day.
Its boards were walls forming places. The ground
holds a trace of a garden. Rusting cars
flourish in the yard. Every place we have been
we have also left. Things fill the land,
detached from some past where their shape had meaning.
The turnouts all along these roads are lush
with beer bottles. Occasionally, we find a diaper, a condom,
intimate and used.
Behind the government fences lie buildings
empty of purpose, though we keep them full of people
to distinguish them from waste,
which sits in tanks underground.
A group of tanks is called a farm.
In 1943, the farmers here were told by mail
to abandon their land in thirty days; fruit hung
on the orchards' trees.
When we step onto the sand outside the car, the car
is empty of people. Some of the tanks in the ground are leaking.
The reactors appear as a cluster of boxes and domes and towers.
The secrets inside are now only artifacts of secrets;
these machines are the residue of fear, eternal
as all trash. Now you are waiting in the car,
patiently or impatiently.
You could drive off without me and risk being only
what you had left behind.

RIDING MOWER, BACKYARD, STEAM CLOUDS FROM PERRY NUCLEAR POWER PLANT, OHIO

There's a science to it, this mowing –
mass of mower, momentum of turn, simple force –
the physics of cut, and I am cutting it all down,
my field of nothing much, shaping the perfect order of grid across
     mounds and dips.
I like the bouncing seat, the unresisting wheel, the snug indentation
to hold a can of beer – the effortless work;
I cannot see the blade. Below, a groundhog hole
bursts into dust, clattering rock and dirt.

My telephone book assures me that everything is made of atoms.
If told to take shelter, I am to strip down,
wash with mild soap, lukewarm water.
If told to evacuate, I am to grab a credit card
and an extra pair of shoes. Some atoms give off radiation.
If the mower stutters, I walk across the yard and get a can of gas.
If the beer is empty, I walk across the yard and get a can of beer –
this prophetic calculation of sequence.

Small puffs of clouds on the horizon
rise through a sunny day. I plant
imaginary trees, planning obstruction –
each leaf absorbing. The mower chews through
a plastic bag. In the case of a simple unusual event,
I am to do nothing.
The mower reaches the edge –
I have nothing to do.

BEAUTY CONTEST: SWEETHEART OF HANFORD ENGINEER WORKS, QUEEN OF SAFETY, 1944

Because of a code of secrecy based on patriotic duty, employees of what was known as Hanford Engineer Works were unaware until after the bomb was dropped that they were building nuclear reactors responsible for manufacturing the plutonium for the bomb used in Nagasaki.

BELLY

The native Bikinians did return briefly, but were evacuated in 1978 after it was made clear that the radioactive effects of the tests still lingered.

PUBLICITY PHOTO, OPERATION CROSSROADS: MUSHROOM CLOUD CAKE

Admiral William H. P. "Spike" Blandy was commander of Operation Crossroads, which in 1946 detonated a number of atomic weapons at Bikini Atoll in an attempt to determine the effect of underwater nuclear explosions on ships and to demonstrate U.S. nuclear technological power. The photograph was titled "Atomic Age Angel Food."

PROJECT CHARIOT: CAPE THOMPSON, ALASKA, 1958

Project Chariot was part of Project Plowshare, which, as the name implies, was a plan to use wartime nuclear technology for peacetime advancements, in this case, blasting a harbor out of Alaska's coast. It never happened, and the studies that led to its cancellation are considered by some to mark the beginning of environmental conservationism.

CANOEING THE HANFORD REACH

The Hanford Reach, a stretch of the Columbia River which runs through the Hanford Nuclear Reservation, is currently designated a National Wild and Scenic River.